Elements Of Grammar And Punctuation In Twelve Lessons

By
Margaret Langfitt

Copyright 2016 by Margaret B. Langfitt
2nd Edition Feb. 2022. All rights reserved.
ISBN: 1544252080 ISBN-13: 978-1544252087

Dedication

To those of you who have a basic knowledge of the correct rules of grammar but who face assaults on the language in everyday conversation and from social media, I dedicate this book, with the hope that the lessons it teaches can keep you from repeating the mistakes of others.

Contents

Introduction...iv

Lesson One: "I" and "Me"...1

Lesson Two: "Who" and "Whom"...5

Lesson Three: Singular or Plural...7

Lesson Four: Adjectives and Adverbs...13

Lesson Five: Comparisons...17

Lesson Six: Prepositions...22

Lesson Seven: The Subjunctive...25

Lesson Eight: "Lie" vs. "Lay"...28

Lesson Nine: Punctuation and Sentence Structure...30

Lesson Ten: More Punctuation...41

Lesson Eleven: Elements of Style...45

Lesson Twelve: Edit Thoroughly...51

*Conclusion...*52

Appendix:

Parts of Speech...53

Sample Sentences...58

Sentence Diagramming...59

Introduction

The invention of the printing press, in the fifteenth century, gave every author access to a larger audience and exposed the need for standardization of language. Over time formal rules for spelling, grammar, and punctuation developed. Today, anyone who wants to communicate effectively should memorize the rules of the language and practice using them until they become second nature.

Lesson One

"I" and "Me"

Most language errors involve the pronouns "I" and "me."

Use "I," Not "Me," After the Verb "To Be"

The verb "to be" expresses a state of being, rather than an action. This makes it a *linking verb*, because it can link two subjects together.

With linking verbs, the noun that follows the verb is not an object, but a second subject, also called the *predicate nominative*. In the following examples, notice that when the predicate nominative (underlined) is a pronoun, it is a subject pronoun, not an object pronoun.

Correct:

    The people coming tonight *are* <u>we</u>.

    The players I like best *are* <u>they</u>.

    The two pairs *are* <u>he and you and Bill and I</u>.

    They think she*'s* <u>I</u>.

    If it *were* <u>I</u>, I would go.

    Why does it always have *to be* <u>I</u> who does the dishes?

    I prefer that the ones doing the dishes *be* <u>he and she</u>.

The subject and the predicate nominative are both subject nouns, so they can switch positions without altering the meaning of the sentence. The only difference between "It is I" and "I am it" is the conjugation of the verb.

Even if you remember to say "It is I," you may still find it hard to say "It is Thomas, Jason, Kent, Angela, John, Michelle, Christopher, Allison, and I." The further the pronoun gets from the verb, the harder it is to recall which form to use.

Even one extra word following the verb can befuddle.

Incorrect:

> It's just me.

Drop the word "just," and the structure of the sentence is clear: *subject – linking verb – predicate nominative*.

Correct:

> It's just I.

Use "Me," not "I," as the Object of a Sentence

In middle school, students learn about linking verbs and struggle to say "It is I" instead of "It is me." From that time forward, young people develop a misplaced fear of ever using the word "me." Do you agree with the use of "I" and "me" in these two examples?

> We are a full group: Tom, John, Jane, and *I*.

> We have a full group: Tom, John, Jane, and *me*.

Both are correct. In the first, the word "group" is a predicate nominative, because it follows the verb "to be," so the subject form of the pronoun is proper when listing its members. In the second example, "group" is a direct object, so "me" is correct.

Incorrect:

> My grandfather often eats lunch with friends and then visits my brother and I.

First, isolate the relevant elements in the second half of the sentence: *my grandfather – visits – [I or me]*. Next, identify their parts of speech: *subject – action verb – direct object*. The pronoun at the end is a direct object, so use "me" instead of "I."

Correct:

> My grandfather often eats lunch with friends and then visits my brother and me.

Can you confirm that every occurrence of the word "I" in the sentences below is a mistake that should be "me"?

Incorrect:

> With you, Matt, and I leading the way, we won't get lost.
>
> Here is a photograph of Dan, Jane, and I at the game.
>
> Tom stands in height between you and I.
>
> My uncle gave my sister and I each a gift to celebrate her and I graduating.

These examples should convince you: do not be afraid to use "me." "Me" can be a direct object, an indirect object, or a prepositional object.

Correct:

> With you, Matt, and *me* leading the way, we won't get lost. (Use "me" after the preposition "with.")
>
> Here is a photograph of Dan, Jane, and *me* at the game. (Use "me" after the preposition "of.")
>
> My uncle gave my sister and *me* each a gift to celebrate her and *me* graduating. (Use "me" as an indirect object in the first occurrence and as a direct object in the second occurrence.)
>
> Tom stands in height between you and *me*. (Use "me" after the preposition "between.")

Use "I," Not "Me," as the Subject of a Sentence

The casual conversation of many well-educated young adults includes a slang form of "me" at the beginning of a sentence.

Incorrect:

> Me and my friend want cake.

This mistake baffles me. I never hear anyone say "Me want cake." The error happens only when the subject includes a second person. Pretend that the other party is not there, and then choose between "me" and "I."

Correct:

I and my friend want cake.

The above is correct grammatically, but it is polite to place yourself last in a list.

My friend and I want cake.

The slang use of an object pronoun at the start of a sentence has expanded beyond "me."

Incorrect:

Him and his brother went to the store.

Again, pretend the other party is not there, and then it is clear that the pronoun at the start of the sentence must be in the subject form.

Correct:

He and his brother went to the store.

Lesson Two

"Who" and "Whom"

After mastering "I" and "me," the next step is to conquer "who" and "whom." "Whom" is the object pronoun of the pair and is just as important as "me" within the structure of a sentence. Why is it, then, that "whom" is largely absent from conversation? Introduce the word "whom" into your vocabulary by following two rules.

1. Use "whom," not "who," as an object pronoun.

2. Use "who" or "whom," but never "that," when referring to a person.

Use "Whom" as the Object Pronoun

Remember the five noun roles, and use "who" as the subject or the predicate nominative and "whom" as the direct object, indirect object, or prepositional object.

Subject: *Who* went?

Predicate Nominative: It is *who*?

Direct Object: *Whom* does he like?

Indirect Object: *Whom* do you give credit for the win?

Prepositional Object: With *whom* did she go?

Can you choose the correct pronoun below?

Who/whom did they hire?

For *who/whom* are you voting?

Correct:

Whom did they hire? (direct object)

For *whom* are you voting? (prepositional object)

Use "Who" or "Whom," not "That," to Indicate a Person

Many speakers avoid choosing between "who" and "whom" by using "that," wrongly, instead. "That" can be either the subject of a sentence or the object, but "that" relates only to plants, animals, and things, not to people, so it is never a correct replacement for "who" or "whom."

Incorrect:

> The candidate that I want to win is leading.

Correct:

> The candidate *whom* I want to win is leading.

Incorrect:

> The students that succeed study diligently.

Correct:

> The students *who* succeed study diligently.

Incorrect:

> He is the one that I trust.

Correct:

> He is the one *whom* I trust.

Surprisingly, I hear this mistake as well in the other direction – the use of "who" instead of "that" to identify a thing.

Incorrect:

> The nations who attended the summit distributed a plan for world peace.

Correct in one of two ways:

> The nations *that* attended the summit distributed a plan for world peace. (Use "that" to refer to "nations.")

> The *diplomats* who attended the summit distributed a plan for world peace. (Use a noun that portrays people.)

Lesson Three

Singular or Plural

The subject of a sentence is either singular or plural, but never both. The rest of the sentence must conform in number with the subject.

The Verb Must Match in Number with the Subject

Most people know this rule and correctly say "he eats" and "they eat." A certain type of noun, though, a quantifying noun, creates confusion.

A quantifying noun takes its number, either singular or plural, from the prepositional phrase that follows it. Examples of quantifying expressions are "a number of," "plenty of," "all of," "lots of," "a lot of," "a bunch of," and "a majority of." In sentences with a quantifying noun, the prepositional object that follows "of" controls whether the subject is singular or plural.

Incorrect:

> A majority of the board favor the candidate.

Correct in one of two ways:

> A majority of the board favors the candidate. (Use a singular verb to match the singular noun "board.")

> A majority of board members favor the candidate. (Make the prepositional object plural to match the plural verb.)

Quantifying nouns often appear in sentences that begin with "there" or "here." The words "there" and "here" are adverbs and do not control whether the sentence is singular or plural.

Incorrect:

> There's a number of students graduating today. ("Students" is plural and needs a plural verb.)

Correct:

> There are a number of students graduating today.

Incorrect:

> Here's a lot of pens in the desk. ("Pens" is plural and needs a plural verb.)

Correct:

> Here are a lot of pens in the desk.

Even when the adverb "there" or "here" does not precede a quantifying noun, the subject and predicate must match in number.

Incorrect:

> There's too many people. ("People" is plural and requires a plural verb.)

Correct:

> There are too many people.

One of the most prolific controversies on the Internet is whether "none" is singular or plural. "None" is short for "no one" or "not one" and within that meaning is singular. On the other hand, the phrase "none of" can be a quantifying expression that adopts its number from the prepositional object.

When used to emphasize "oneness," "none" is singular.

> Not a single one of the projects is complete.

> None is complete.

When used as a quantifying noun, "none" can be plural.

> A bunch of his friends were here yesterday, but none [of his friends] are here today.

The expression "not any" is synonymous with "none" and, like "none," is singular when emphasizing "oneness" but can be plural when used as a quantifying noun.

Not any of the hats in all the stores is pink. (Not any [one] – is – pink.)

There are a lot of red buttons, but not any are pink. (Not any [of the buttons] – are – pink.)

The expressions "not one," "everyone," "neither," and "either" are always singular. These never function as quantifying nouns even when followed by the preposition "of."

Correct:

She has a lot of hats, but not one of them fits me.

Everyone is going to love it.

Neither of her parents is going to the game.

Either of them is allowed.

Direct Objects Must Match Within the Sentence

Incorrect:

Bob and Joe put their shoulder to the task.

Correct:

Bob and Joe put their *shoulders* to the task.

Incorrect:

Their actions now will affect their entire life.

Correct:

Their actions now will affect their entire *lives*.

Indirect Objects Must Match Within the Sentence

Incorrect:

All campers write their mother.

Correct:

All campers write their *mothers*.

Prepositional Objects Must Match Within the Sentence

Incorrect:

> The class taught them to come out of their comfort zone.

Correct:

> The class taught them to come out of their comfort *zones*.

A Noun and Its Modifier Must Match in Number

Most adjectives are number neutral. You can have a thirsty dog or thirsty dogs, for example. Those few adjectives that are number specific must match the nouns they modify.

Incorrect:

> Less people are in attendance. ("Less" is singular, so it does not match with the plural noun "people.")

Correct in one of two ways:

> *Fewer* people are in attendance. (Use a plural adjective.)

> There is less *attendance*. (Use a singular noun.)

Incorrect:

> Other people have less problems. ("Less" does not match with "problems.")

Correct in one of two ways:

> Other people have *fewer* problems. (Use "fewer.")

> Other people have less *worry*. (Use a singular noun.)

Incorrect:

> How much dollars do you have? ("Much" is singular, so it cannot describe the plural noun "dollars.")

Correct in one of two ways:

> How *many* dollars do you have? (Use the plural modifier.)

> How much *money* do you have? (Use a singular noun.)

The same error occurs when "much" and "less" act as nouns.

Incorrect:

> Much of the shirts sold, so less are left. ("Much" and "less" do not fit within a plural sentence.)

Correct in one of two ways:

> *Many* of the shirts sold, so *fewer* are left. (Make the sentence plural.)

> Much of the *merchandise* sold, so less is left. (Make the sentence singular.)

A Noun and Its Pronoun Must Match in Number

Incorrect:

> Everyone needs to improve their game.

Correct in one of two ways:

> Everyone needs to improve *his or her* game. (Use singular pronouns to reference the singular noun "everyone.")

> *All players* need to improve their games. (Make the subject plural.)

Incorrect:

> Each player needs to register, so they can pick up their uniform.

Correct in one of two ways:

> Each player needs to register, so *he or she* can pick up *his or her* uniform. (Use singular pronouns to match the singular subject.)

> *All players* need to register, so they can pick up their uniforms. (Make the subject plural.)

Incorrect:

> That an artist's work can effectively represent them is a beautiful concept.

Correct in one of two ways:

> That an artist's work can effectively represent *him* or *her* is a beautiful concept. (Use singular pronouns to match the singular noun "artist.")
>
> That *artists' work* can effectively represent them is a beautiful concept. (Make the noun plural.)

Lesson Four

Adjectives and Adverbs

Two rules control the use of modifiers: (1) use an adjective to describe a noun or a pronoun; (2) use an adverb to modify all other parts of speech.

> It is way too loud.

"Loud" describes "it" and is the only adjective. "Too" and "way" are adverbs that describe "loud" and "too."

Some modifiers can function as either an adjective or an adverb.

> The well child may stay. ("Well" is an adjective.)
>
> The child well may stay. ("Well" is an adverb.)

Placement can affect meaning.

> The fancy new dog's leash is made of leather. (The dog is fancy and new.)
>
> The dog's fancy new leash is made of leather. (The leash is fancy and new.)
>
> I met the young boss's spouse at the party. (The boss is young.)
>
> I met the boss's young spouse at the party. (The spouse is young.)

How to Use Comparative and Superlative Modifiers

Modifiers that compare members in a group are either *comparative*, for groups of two, or *superlative*, for groups of three or more. In most cases, form the comparative and superlative by adding the suffix "-er" or "-est" to the modifier.

Exceptions include adjectives with more than two syllables, adjectives ending in "-ful" or "-less," and adverbs ending in "-ly."

For these exceptions, form the comparative or superlative by preceding the modifier with "less," "more," "least," or "most".

Correct:

> Which mattress on these twin beds is *less comfortable*?
>
> He jumps *highest*, swims *fastest*, and runs *most quickly*.
>
> College is *harder* and *more stressful* than high school.

Other exceptions are "better," "best," "worse," and "worst," which are the comparative and superlative forms of "good," "well," "bad," and "badly."

> He tries *harder,* but she plays *better*.
>
> Our team's *best* player is *worse* than their *worst*.

A frequent mistake is to use a superlative modifier, instead of the comparative, in a comparison of two.

Incorrect:

> Between him and her, I don't know whom I hate most.

Correct:

> Between him and her, I don't know whom I hate *more*.

Incorrect:

> Who is fastest, you or I?

Correct:

> Who is *faster*, you or I?

Use Adverbs, not Adjectives, to Describe Verbs

Incorrect:

> Janet ran quick.

Correct:

> Janet ran *quickly*.

Incorrect:

> Do you view the candidate different since the election?

Correct:

> Do you view the candidate *differently* since the election?

Incorrect:

> She did good in today's lesson. ("Good" is an adjective, so it can never describe a verb.)

Correct:

> She did well in today's lesson. (Use "well" instead, because "well" can be either an adjective or an adverb.)

Roadside warnings that tell us to "Drive safe" should say "Drive safely." The motto "Live fearless" needs an adverb: "Live fearlessly."

The same mistake occurs with comparative and superlative modifiers. To describe a verb, use the adverb form.

Incorrect:

> The corn grows slower than the beans. (Instead of "slow," use the adverb "slowly" to describe the verb "grows.")

Correct:

> The corn grows *more slowly* than the beans.

Use Adjectives with Linking Verbs

Linking verbs link the modifier back to the subject. Follow a linking verb with an adjective or adjective phrase that describes the subject.

Correct:

> She was *good* in the lesson.
>
> The cake tastes *delicious*.
>
> He looks *like a movie star*.

The piano sounds *out of tune*.

The first sentence below uses a linking verb and an adjective to express a state of being. The second uses the same verb, plus an adverb, to describe an action.

- Correct:

> Sue *feels strong* enough to leave the hospital.
>
> Sue *feels strongly* about staying healthy.

What is the difference between the following sentences?

> Jan feels bad.
>
> Jan feels badly.

The first means that Jan is sick or upset. The second means that she is unable to feel things with her fingers.

> Sam smells bad.
>
> Sam smells badly.

The first means he needs to take a shower; the second means his olfactory system is inadequate.

In the sentences below, the first uses "stand" as an action verb, and the second uses it as a linking verb.

Correct:

> The soldiers stand silently.
>
> The soldiers stand firm.

The following sentence uses the verb "run" as both an action verb and a linking verb. Can you tell which is which?

> When a clock runs slow, its gears run too slowly.

Lesson Five

Comparisons

There are two types of comparisons:

(1) those that use a conjunction to compare two clauses and

(2) those that use a preposition to compare two nouns.

When writing a comparison, keep in mind the following rules:

(1) compare things that are logically comparable,

(2) use correct pronouns within parallel clauses, and

(3) do not rely on parallelism between clauses when using the adjective "different" or the adverb "differently."

Comparisons that Use a Conjunction

A conjunction joins two clauses into one sentence. A clause is a phrase that has both a subject and a predicate. Use "than" or "as" as conjunctions to juxtapose two clauses.

Correct:

Sue is as tall as *I am*.

Sue ran the race faster than *I did*.

Tim talks more than *he listens*.

Joe plays tennis better than *he plays squash*.

The use of a conjunction in a comparison forces a parallel structure between the clauses, and the parallelism permits you to drop the redundant elements of the second clause.

Equally correct:

Sue is as tall as *I*.

Sue ran the race faster than *I*.

Tim talks more than *listens*.

Joe plays tennis better than *squash.*

In the sentences below, can you identify the elements of the first clause that have dropped from the second clause?

I like him better than her.

I like him better than she.

The first example compares the object pronouns "him" and "her." Both the subject and the predicate drop from the second clause. It means that I like him better than [I like] her.

The second example compares the subject pronouns "I" and "she." Both the predicate and the object drop from the second clause. It means that I like him better than she [likes him].

Comparisons that Use a Preposition

The second type of comparison uses a preposition, "to" or "from," to contrast two nouns. The two nouns are the subject of the sentence and the prepositional object that follows "to" or "from."

Your large cat is equal to my small dog in weight.

Your hat is similar to one that I own.

My dress is different from yours.

The Comparison Must Be Logical

You can compare two nouns or two clauses, but never compare a noun with a clause.

Incorrect:

The lecture James gave was longer than Tyler gave.

Correct in one of two ways:

The lecture James gave was longer than the lecture Tyler gave. (Compare two lectures.)

James lectured longer than Tyler did. (Compare two clauses.)

Incorrect:

The lunch she ate was longer than I swam. (This wrongly compares the noun "lunch" with the clause "I swam.")

Correct in one of two ways:

The lunch she ate was longer than my swim. (Compare the length of the lunch with the length of the swim.)

She ate lunch longer than I swam. (Compare two clauses.)

Incorrect:

My cat's weight is equal to my dog. (The nouns "weight" and "dog" are not logically comparable.)

Correct in one of two ways:

My cat's weight is equal to my dog's, (Compare the two animals' weights.)

My cat in weight is equal to my dog. (Compare two animals.)

Use a Pronoun that Maintains the Parallel Structure

In comparisons that use the conjunction "than" or "as," the two sides of the comparison must contain equivalent structures.

Incorrect:

They are as good as us. (The subject pronoun "they" and the object pronoun "us" are not equivalent.)

She is better than me. (The subject pronoun "she" and the object pronoun "me" are not equivalent.)

He plays as well as them both. (The subject pronoun "he" and the object pronoun "them" are not equivalent.)

The right side of each of the above sentences needs a subject-form pronoun to match the structure on the left side.

Correct:

They are as good as *we [are]*. (Replace "us" with "we.")

She is better than *I [am]*. (Replace "me" with "I.")

He plays as well as *they* both *[play]*. (Replace "them" with "they.")

How to Use "Different" in a Comparison

The modifier "different" is unique because it can precede either the conjunction "than" or the preposition "from." In other words, "different" can be used in either type of comparison.

Common use of the phrase "different from" to compare two nouns makes the parallelism associated with "different than" too weak to support a silent noun or verb in the second clause. Therefore, when using the phrase "different than," use a full clause on both sides of the conjunction. If you prefer to drop the second verb, then change the conjunction "than" to the preposition "from," and, when a pronoun follows "from," change the subject form to the object.

Urban living is different than *rural living is*. (Use a full clause on both sides.)

Urban living is different *from rural living*. (To drop the second verb, change "than" to "from.")

My father is different than *I am*. (Use two full clauses.)

My father is different *from me*. (To drop the second verb, change "than" to "from" and "I" to "me.")

Remember that conjunctions compare clauses by joining them into one sentence. Each side of the sentence must have a subject and a predicate. To compare two nouns, on the other hand, use a prepositional phrase.

The soup today is different than *it is* usually. (Use a full clause in the second half of the sentence.)

The soup today is different *from the usual soup*. (Use a prepositional phrase to complete the comparison.)

The weather today is different than *it was* last night. (Use a full clause.)

The weather today is different *from the weather* last night. (Use a prepositional phrase.)

The same rule applies to the adverb "differently." Use either "than" or "from," but be sure to complete the parallelism when comparing two clauses.

They play the game differently than *we do*. (Use "than" to compare the two clauses "they play" and "we do.")

They play the game differently *from us*. (Use "from" to compare the subject "they" with the prepositional object "us.")

Can you hear the error in the following two examples?

Incorrect:

Meg is different than me.

She behaves differently than me.

Correct either by using a full clause on the second side of the conjunction or by replacing "than" with the preposition "from."

Correct:

Meg is different than *I am*.

Meg is different *from me*.

She behaves differently than *I do*.

She behaves differently *from me*.

Lesson Six

Prepositions

A preposition defines the relationship between words in a sentence, such as "the hat *on* the shelf" or "the man *from* Arizona."

"Between" vs. "Among"

Use "between" when there are two in a group and "among" when there are three or more.

> I stood *between* my friends, and we chatted *among* ourselves.

When using "between," the modifier "two" is redundant.

> I parked between the two lines. (redundant)

> I parked between the lines. (Drop the "two.")

How do the following sentences differ?

> There is much squabbling between the brothers and the sister.

> There is much squabbling among the brothers and the sister.

The first means that the brothers as a unit squabble with the sister. The second means that all squabble with one another.

"Of" vs. "Have"

"Of" is a preposition; "have" is a verb. When writing "could've" or any similar contraction, use "have," not "of."

Incorrect:

> I could of won.

Correct:

> I could *have* won.

Avoid Ending a Sentence with a Preposition

The word *preposition* means "positioned before." A preposition must come *before* an object and, therefore, should never end a sentence. If a preposition does end a sentence, then the preposition and its object do not adjoin.

Incorrect:

> What are you looking for?

Correct:

> *For what* are you looking?

Incorrect:

> Which party are you going to?

Correct:

> *To which party* are you going?

When the prepositional object is a person, use *whom*, not *who*.

Incorrect:

> Who are you looking for?

Correct:

> *For whom* are you looking?

If you can drop the final preposition entirely without altering the meaning of the sentence, then do so.

Incorrect:

> Where are we going to eat at?

Correct:

> Where are we going to eat? (Drop the preposition.)

What do you think of the following sentence?

> I didn't want to.

Yes, the word "to" is a preposition, and, as such, cannot end a sentence. In this construction, though, "to" does not function as a preposition. It serves as the beginning of an infinitive. The remainder of the infinitive is silent. When "to" is not acting as a preposition, then it does not need an object and, therefore, may end a sentence.

> I went, although I didn't want to [go].

> I ate a lot, but I didn't mean to [eat a lot].

Words that are prepositions can behave as adverbs. If a word that is usually a preposition operates instead as an adverb, then it does not have a prepositional object, and it may end the sentence.

> Come *in*. ("In" describes the verb "come.")

> Carry *on*. ("On" describes the verb "carry.")

"Try To" vs. "Try And"

Use "try to" to designate the single action of *trying to do something*.

Incorrect:

> Try and win.

Correct:

> Try *to* win.

"Talk With" vs. "Talk To"

In conversation, you speak or talk *with* someone. When you lecture, you talk *to* an audience.

> I spoke with my children to get their input.

> I spoke to my students about their behavior.

Lesson Seven

The Subjunctive

Think of the subjunctive as mixing philosophy and grammar: something can't *be* if it *isn't*. In every use of the subjunctive, the expected tense of the verb changes to show that something *is not* happening. For example, "I wish it is raining" is incorrect. Do not use the normal indicative tense unless it is in fact raining. Instead, use the subjunctive: "I wish it *were* raining."

Create the subjunctive in any dependent clause that follows the verb "wish" by using the past tense of the verb instead of the usual indicative tense.

Incorrect:

> I wish that he understands.

Correct:

> I wish that he understood. (Use past tense.)

If the dependent clause contains the verb "to be," which is the only verb in the English language that has multiple conjugations in the past tense, then use the past-tense third-person plural conjugation.

Incorrect:

> He is hungry and wishes he is at dinner.

Correct:

> He is hungry and wishes he *were* at dinner. (With "to be," use "were.")

Use the same form of the subjunctive in a dependent clause that follows or precedes the word "would" or "could."

Incorrect:

Could you go if I find the tickets?

Correct:

Could you go if I *found* the tickets? (Use past tense to create the subjunctive.)

Incorrect:

If I am sick, I would stay home.

Correct:

If I *were* sick, I would stay home. (With "to be," use "were.")

In a dependent clause that follows an action of contingency, such as suggesting, demanding, asking, or insisting, form the subjunctive by using the verb's simple infinitive instead of the indicative conjugation.

Incorrect:

I requested that he provided a sample. ("Provided" is the matching indicative tense, but the action is contingent, so replace the indicative with the subjunctive.)

Correct:

I requested that he *provide* a sample. (Use the infinitive to form the subjunctive.)

Incorrect:

I ask that she is quiet. (Do not use the indicative tense.)

Correct:

I ask that she *be* quiet. (Use the infinitive.)

The subjunctive creates a unique mood that no other tense can match. If you choose, however, to forego the subjunctive, you can do so by changing the sentence structure.

Equally correct:

I wish *for understanding.* (Remove the dependent clause.)

26

He is hungry and wishes *to eat*. (Remove the dependent clause.)

Can you go if I find the tickets? (Use "can" instead of "could.")

If I am ill, I *will* stay home. (Use "will" instead of "would.")

I requested *a sample*. (Remove the dependent clause.)

I ask *for quiet*. (Remove the dependent clause.)

Lesson Eight

"Lie" vs. "Lay"

"To lie" and "to lay" are separate verbs, but people confuse them because they sound similar and have similar meanings. The verb "lie" means to rest or to sleep. The verb "lay" means to put, rest, or place something somewhere.

It is easy to tell "lie" and "lay" apart in a sentence because "to lie" is an intransitive verb (one that does not have a direct object) and "to lay" is a transitive verb (one that requires a direct object).

> I lie on the couch. ("Lie" is an intransitive verb, so it does not have a direct object.)
>
> I lay the book on the table. ("Lay" is a transitive verb, and "book" is the direct object.)

The three principal forms of a verb are the present tense, the past tense, and the past participle. For "lie," these are "lie," "lay," and "lain." For "lay," they are "lay," "laid," and "laid."

Can you identify the verb and tense in each sentence below?

> I lie down. (Present tense of "lie.")
>
> I lay down. (Past tense of "lie.")
>
> I lay myself down. (Present tense of "lay.")
>
> I laid myself down. (Past tense of "lay.")

The confusion between "to lie" and "to lay" arises mainly with the word "laid." "Laid" is the past tense of "to lay," but speakers frequently misuse it as the past tense of "to lie." In other words, people often say "laid" when they should say "lay."

Correct:

> I *laid* the balls on the table, racked them up and broke them, then studied where they *lay*.
>
> I wanted to *lay* the bags on the table, but my papers *lay* there already, so instead I *laid* the bags on the chair.
>
> The pencils that my son *laid* on the table earlier are still lying there now as I *lay* the pens next to them.

Read the following passage published in *White-Jacket* by Herman Melville.

Incorrect:

> Often I have lain thus, when the fact, that if I laid much longer I would actually freeze to death, would come over me with such overpowering force as to break the icy spell, and starting to my feet, I would endeavor to go through the combined manual and pedal exercise to restore the circulation.

First, notice the verb "have lain," which is a correct use of the past participle form of "to lie." Next, look closely at the word "laid." This use cannot be correct because "laid" must have a direct object and does not. The context shows that Melville intended to use "lay," the subjunctive form of "to lie," because the verb appears in a dependent clause that precedes the word "would." Therefore, the correct choice is "lay," not "laid."

This mistake is common. If you use the word "laid," consider whether you mean to say "lay" instead.

Correct:

> Often I have lain thus, when the fact, that if I *lay* much longer I would actually freeze to death, would come over me with such overpowering force as to break the icy spell, and starting to my feet, I would endeavor to go through the combined manual and pedal exercise to restore the circulation.

Lesson Nine

Punctuation and Sentence Structure

Punctuation is a signal from writer to reader that indicates when to pause and what to emphasize.

>Come on. Keep up.

>Come on! Keep up!

>Come on; keep up.

>Come on, keep up.

In every clause above, the subject is the word "you," which is the silent but implied subject of every command. The changes in punctuation reflect differences when speaking and, in the last two examples, indicate a *compound sentence* and a *compound predicate*.

Compound Predicates

A compound predicate is two or more verbs that apply to the same noun. Join the verbs with a comma alone, a conjunction alone, or a comma plus a conjunction. The conjunctions available for this use are "and," "but," "yet," "or," "nor," "for," and "so."

>Tom swims, bikes, jogs all in one day.

>I will not swim, nor jog.

>I stayed for dinner but left before dessert.

Compound Subjects

A compound subject is two or more nouns that relate to the same verb. The rules that create a compound predicate also create a compound subject.

Correct:

Tom, Kate, Carol met for dinner. (join with a comma alone)

Tom and Kate and Carol met for dinner. (join with a conjunction alone)

Tom, Kate, and Carol met for dinner. (join with a comma plus a conjunction)

If the compound subject includes both singular and plural nouns, then the noun nearest the verb controls the number.

The dog or the cats have to go. (The verb matches *cats*.)

The meat and potatoes or the casserole or the soup makes a good meal. (The verb matches *soup*.)

If commas surround part of a compound subject, then that part cannot control the verb.

The furniture, but not the rug or the curtains, is staying. (The verb matches *furniture*.)

Tim, so also his children are here. (The commas do not enclose the second noun, so the verb matches *children*.)

Compound Objects

The same rules that create a compound predicate or subject also create a compound object.

We prefer eggs, cereal, or yogurt.

I saw Tim, yet not his wife.

I saw my infant niece, for also her mother at the party.

Coordinating Conjunctions and Compound Sentences

The seven conjunctions that can create compound predicates, subjects, and objects – "and," "but," "yet," "or," "nor," "for," and "so" – are *coordinating conjunctions*. They join two independent structures, and neither structure is subordinate.

A *compound sentence* is one that combines two independent structures where each structure is a clause. Join the clauses with a comma plus a coordinating conjunction, with a semicolon, or with a colon.

Correct:

> We talked late into the night, so I am tired today.
>
> I hear that you have been seeing someone who has no job and no prospects; that is your own business.
>
> I have an idea: let's go swimming!

Combining independent clauses without correct punctuation results in an error called a "run-on" sentence.

Incorrect:

> Jane ate and then she and Tom left. (A conjunction alone cannot join sentences.)

Still incorrect:

> Jane ate, then she and Tom left. (A comma alone cannot join sentences.)

Correct:

> Jane ate, and then she and Tom left. (Use both a comma and a conjunction to form a compound sentence.)

"However," "therefore," "thus," and "then" are not conjunctions. They are adverbs and cannot join sentences.

Incorrect:

> I tasted the pie, however I prefer it without nuts. (This is a run-on sentence.)

Correct:

> I tasted the pie, but I prefer it without nuts. (Replace "however" with a coordinating conjunction.)

Also correct:

> I tasted the pie. However, I prefer it without nuts. (Make it two sentences.)

A clause that begins with a coordinating conjunction cannot stand alone as a sentence.

Incorrect:

> But I don't want to go.

Correct:

> I could go, but I don't want to go.

Subordinating Conjunctions and Complex Sentences

Many other conjunctions exist, besides the seven coordinating conjunctions. All others are *subordinating conjunctions* because they create subordinate, or dependent, clauses. Examples of subordinating conjunctions are "while," "since," "if," "because," "when," "as," "where," "although," "whether," and "after."

There are three types of dependent clauses: adverb clauses, noun clauses, and adjective clauses. A *complex sentence* is one that contains at least one dependent clause.

> I vote for her *because she is local*. (adverb clause)

> I vote for *whoever is local*. (noun clause)

> I vote for the candidate *who is local*. (adjective clause)

The first example uses a subordinating conjunction – "because" – to join the dependent clause to the main clause. Each clause in the three examples, whether it is the main clause or the dependent clause, contains both a subject and a predicate.

Adverb Clauses

An adverb clause describes the verb by answering the question "why," "where," "when," or "how." The only way to create an adverb clause is with a subordinating conjunction.

> We cooked dinner *after we went shopping*.

> He made the salad and set the table *while I fixed the meat*.

> We arrived *when the doors were closing*.

> *As I waited for the doctor*, twelve new patients walked in.

The conjunction within an adverb clause may be silent if context implies it.

> She talks about the scarcity of water, which is, she correctly states, a problem in many nations.
>
> She talks about the scarcity of water, which is, [as] she correctly states, a problem in many nations.

An adverb clause can begin a sentence but cannot stand alone as a sentence.

Incorrect:

> Because it rained.

Correct by inserting a main clause either before or after the subordinate clause.

> We stopped because it rained.
>
> Because it rained, we stopped.

Noun Clauses

A noun clause replaces a noun and turns a simple sentence into a complex sentence.

> He travels with his son. (simple sentence)
>
> He travels with whomever he wants. (complex sentence)

A noun clause can begin with a pronoun, as in the above example, or with a subordinating conjunction.

Pronouns that can begin a noun clause are "what," "which," "who," "whom," "whose," "whoever," and "whomever."

> Think about *what you want*.
>
> *Which destination they pick* depends on the weather.

The pronoun plays a role within the clause, so use the pronoun that fits the role. Most errors involve the mistaken use of "who" instead of "whom."

Incorrect:

> The best player is *who I want*. (The dependent clause needs a direct object, so use "whom.")

Correct:

> The best player is *whom I want.*
>
> *For whom Susan will vote* is her decision.
>
> *Whomever you choose* may come.
>
> I shall give *whoever has the best voice* the star role.
>
> Open the door for *whoever comes first.*

A subordinating conjunction, such as "that," "if," "whether," "why," "where," "when," or "how," also can create a noun clause.

> *That they didn't win* is a tragedy.
>
> I don't know *if I am going.*
>
> *Whether I go* will be a last-minute decision.
>
> *Why he is here* is a mystery.
>
> *Where we eat* is your choice.
>
> You choose *when we shall eat.*
>
> Teach your children *how they should behave.*

The conjunction may be silent when introducing a direct object.

> She hopes *she will win.*
>
> She hopes *[that] she will win.*

Adjective Clauses

An adjective clause differs from a noun clause because it describes the noun but does not replace it.

> *Whoever is ready* will go next. (noun clause)
>
> The one *who is ready* will go next. (adjective clause)

An adjective clause must describe a noun within the same sentence.

Incorrect:

She takes the exam tomorrow. Which has been a struggle for many.

Those were the best days of our lives. When we were young and carefree.

Correct by creating adjective clauses.

She takes the exam, which has been a struggle for many, tomorrow.

Those days, when we were young and carefree, were the best of our lives.

An adjective clause can begin with either a pronoun, such as "that," "which," "who," "whom," or "whose," or with a modifier, such as "why," "where," or "when." These are called *relative* pronouns and modifiers because they relate back to the noun being described.

I remember the day *that we met*. (relative pronoun)

I salute the friend *who introduced us*. (relative pronoun)

I have a friend *whom you know*. (relative pronoun).

I remember the time *when we met*. (relative modifier)

I remember the place *where we met*. (relative modifier)

A relative pronoun that acts as a direct object may be silent.

The man *she is dating* just arrived.

The man *[whom] she is dating* just arrived.

When a relative pronoun references a person, such as "who," "whom," and "whose," choose the pronoun that fits within the clause.

The candidate <u>who</u> *won the primary* is now in the general election. (The clause uses the pronoun as its subject.)

The friend *with <u>whom</u> I live* leaves next month. (The clause uses the pronoun as a prepositional object.)

The farmer *whose property this is* lives across the street. (The clause requires the possessive pronoun.)

The relative pronouns "which" and "that" identify animals, plants, or things. These two pronouns are not interchangeable. Use "which" if the clause contains extraneous information and separate the clause from the rest of the sentence with commas. Use "that" if the clause controls meaning and do not separate it from the rest of the sentence.

The dog, *which* is outside, will come in later to eat. (With extraneous information, use "which" and use commas to separate the clause from the rest of the sentence.)

The dog *that* is outside eats later than the others. (With essential information, use "that" and do not separate.)

Punctuation of Modifiers

The same rule about when to use "which" or "that" as a relative pronoun in an adjective clause applies to punctuation of all modifiers. Use commas only if the modifier contains extraneous detail. If the modifier provides information that is essential to the meaning of the sentence, then do not enclose it in commas.

The employee whose job I want is leaving the company. (essential information)

The ambassadors, who are staying here, arrived today. (extraneous information)

I like the place where we ate. (essential)

My friend, with whom I studied, did better than I on the exam. (extraneous)

I bought the red book. (essential)

The restaurant, which is near my home, is one of the best in the city. (extraneous)

The book, red, is on the shelf. (extraneous)

The horse that won is mine. (essential)

If you are unsure whether the information within a modifier is essential, consider whether the reader should pause. A comma is an invitation to pause and indicates expendable information.

> Last month, when the pool was open, we swam every day. (extraneous information.)
>
> Although I could not fix the door, I did fix the leak. (extraneous information.)
>
> Do not swim after you eat. (essential information)
>
> I arrived before you did. (essential information)

The presence or absence of commas can alter meaning. From the punctuation below, tell me how many times Ann has married and how many brothers she has.

> When Ann married, in 1996, her brother, John, attended.

The commas tell us that the modifiers "in 1996" and "John" are extra details. Therefore, this is Ann's only marriage, and John is her only brother.

To show that Ann has married more than once and has more than one brother, simply remove the enclosing commas.

> When Ann married in 1996, her brother John attended.

Prepositional Phrases

A prepositional phrase contains both a preposition and a prepositional object and participates in the sentence as either an adjective or adverb.

To determine when to enclose the prepositional phrase in commas, use the same rule that applies to all modifiers.

> That book on the first shelf, *with the blue cover*, is a favorite. (adjective phrase, enclose with commas because this is extraneous information)
>
> I bought it *from the local bookstore*. (adverb phrase, eliminate commas because this is primary information)

Appositives

An appositive is a noun or noun phrase that functions as an adjective. When the appositive contains essential information, it is a *restrictive appositive* and appears without commas. If the appositive contains extraneous information, it is *nonrestrictive* and enclosed in commas.

> I cook separately for my friend *the vegetarian*. (restrictive)
>
> The bird, *a nightingale*, sings beautifully. (nonrestrictive)
>
> My brother *the water skier* owns a boat. (restrictive)
>
> My brother, *a water skier*, owns a boat. (nonrestrictive)

When Is a Modifier "Dangling"?

A modifier that does not clearly reference a specific word within the sentence is "dangling."

Incorrect:

> There is some cake on the plate that my mom made. (Did my mom make the plate or the cake?)
>
> With one week to go before retiring, the company celebrated her long career. (Is the company retiring?)
>
> At the age of ten, my family got its first pet. (Did the family turn ten?)
>
> Ill with mange and emaciated, I gave the dog a medicinal bath and food. (Do I have mange? Am I emaciated?)
>
> While jogging yesterday, the shoes I wore squeaked. (Did the shoes jog?)

Correct:

> There is some cake, which my mom made, on the plate.
>
> With one week to go before her retirement, the company celebrated her long career.
>
> When I turned ten, my family got its first pet.
>
> I gave the dog, ill with mange and emaciated, a medicinal bath and food.

While jogging yesterday, I wore shoes that squeaked.

When is a Pronoun "Dangling"?

The usual rule is that a pronoun relates to the nearest preceding noun, but the greater rule is that the reference must be clear.

> The cookies baked by the students were burned, so we sent them back.

The pronoun "them" refers to the closest prior noun, which is "students," but rewrite the sentence to make it clear.

> The cookies baked by the students were burned, so we sent the students back to try again.

The sentences below lack clarity. Can you rewrite them?

> Mr. Smith will be meeting Mr. Jones, and he is planning to meet other people too.

> Sue told Joan that her foot was hurting.

> Did you see the moon last night at its height?

> The bandage containing the blood reddened as it spread.

> He taught his brother chess when he was home.

Lesson Ten

More Punctuation

The Serial Comma

The serial comma is the last comma in a list of three or more items. British usage drops the serial comma, but writers in America keep it.

> For lunch, I had bread, cheese and fruit. (England)

> For lunch, I had bread, cheese, and fruit. (America)

The Hyphen

When two or more words create a single adjective, hyphenate them.

> The ball fell into the right-corner pocket.

> The blue-popsicle vendor sells to two-year-old children.

When two or more words create a single noun, then you may hyphenate or not, but avoid ambiguity.

> I prefer *orange-juice* instead of *apple juice*.

> The *centerpiece* is an *ice statue*.

> The *ice-bucket* is on the *countertop*.

The Apostrophe

When turning a singular noun into a possessive, always add both an apostrophe and an "s," even when the noun ends in an "s." If a plural noun ends in an "s," then make it possessive by adding only an apostrophe.

> Mr. Jones's car is blue.

> The men's league plays on Saturdays.

> The Johnsons' house is for sale.

Do not confuse *it's, you're* and *who's* with *its, your* and *whose*. The former are contractions that contain a subject and a verb, and the latter are possessive modifiers.

>*You're* driving *your* car.
>
>*Who's* riding in *whose car?*
>
>*It's* a good idea to check *its* tires before starting.

In a contraction, an apostrophe replaces a letter or a series of letters. Apostrophes also can replace numbers. For example, it is correct to contract 1980s into '80s.

Apostrophes help to form a plural when needed for clarification.

>Mind your Do's and Don'ts.
>
>The DVDs are here.
>
>The Yes's outnumber the No's.
>
>I got two Cs, two Bs, and three B-'s.

When making a number plural, add "s," but do not add an apostrophe.

>The decade of the 1960s enjoyed a renaissance in music.

Quotation Marks and Punctuation

The rule in America is to keep a comma or a period inside the final quotation mark, put a semicolon or a colon outside the quotation mark, and put an exclamation mark or a question mark either inside or outside depending on what makes sense.

Correct:

>"I am ready to go," she said.
>
>She said, "I am ready to go."
>
>She said, "I am ready to go"; she was exhausted.
>
>She asked, "Which way do you enter?"
>
>Did she say "Enter to the left"?

She yelled, "Watch out!"

Avoid adjacent punctuation.

Incorrect:

"Does she eat chicken?," she asked.

"Slow down!," she yelled.

Correct:

"Does she eat chicken?" she asked.

"Slow down!" she yelled.

The preference against adjacent marks of punctuation has exceptions. Punctuation that is part of a name (Yahoo!), or part of a title (*Who's Afraid of Virginia Woolf?*), or part of an abbreviation (a.m. or p.m.) may require adjoining punctuation. The following examples illustrate both the rule and its exceptions.

Correct:

"I work at Yahoo!," she said.

She works at Yahoo!

He said, "Many of my neighbors work at Yahoo!"

Do you work at Yahoo!?

Who yelled "Fire!"?

Who starred in *Who's Afraid of Virginia Woolf?*

He starred in *Who's Afraid of Virginia Woolf?*

Do we have to get up at 4:00 a.m.?

We have to get up at 4:00 a.m.

She gasped, "4:00 a.m.!"

She ends every email with "Best Wishes!"

Does she end every email with "Best Wishes!"?

Punctuation within a parenthetical does not count as punctuation outside the parenthetical.

Correct:

> She works in California (at Yahoo!).
>
> You are going to miss the deadline (3:00 p.m.).
>
> She used her usual ending ("Best Wishes!").

Abbreviations

In formal writing, the only permitted abbreviations are a.m., p.m., those that are part of a legal name, and those that shorten dates, common titles, large numbers, or specific times.

Incorrect:

> I live in the U.S.

Correct:

> I live in the United States, in Biloxi, Mississippi, at 1500 First Street.
>
> The party is the last Friday in January at Mr. Jenkins's home at five o'clock p.m.
>
> I was born on July 9, 1961, at 11:36 a.m.
>
> The salad has lettuce, onions, olives, *et cetera*.
>
> I work at Capital Partners, Inc.

When writing the year as a number, separate it with commas if it follows the date of the month.

> After living for many years in Texas, I moved in April 1990 to Florida.
>
> After living for many years in Texas, I moved on April 3, 1990, to Florida.

Lesson Eleven

Elements of Style

Choose your own style, but adhere to the following guidelines.

Be Concise

Determine what you want to accomplish and ensure that every step brings you closer to that goal. For example, get to the point promptly by rejecting empty adverbs like "really," "truly," and "actually." Change "completely unanimous" to "unanimous" and "difficult dilemma" to "dilemma."

The following phrases are expendable.

>In my opinion...
>
>I believe that...
>
>It seems that...
>
>Personally, I...

Strike any modifier that creates a redundancy.

>The young senator is 25 years old. (Drop "young.")
>
>I love my furry, soft, divine, heavenly, and lovable new kitten. (Discard either "heavenly" or the synonymous "divine," and do not use "lovable" with "love.")

Avoid passive voice.

>Passive: The book was written by my sister.
>
>Active: My sister wrote the book.
>
>Passive: The show was admired by all who saw it.
>
>Active: All who saw it admired the show.

Wherever possible, replace "to be," which is the most common verb in the English language, with an action verb.

> My name is Ishmael.

With a simple adjustment Melville creates the memorable first line of his novel *Moby Dick*.

> Call me Ishmael.

The passage below wilts from over-used verbs.

> Reading this book was fun. It has some good information. It didn't take long.

Revive it by improving verb choice and using explicit modifiers.

> Readers who discover this book will find it humorous, informative, and concise.

Limit your use of "there" and "here" to begin a sentence.

> There is much damage in the cities hit by the storm.

> Here is the cat.

Descriptive verbs sharpen the message.

> Much damage *imperils* the cities hit by the storm.

> The cat *approaches*.

Do not use the same word multiple times within a short space.

> I was home last night because it rained, but the night was boring because the nighttime television was boring.

Rewrite to eliminate repetition.

> The rain last night kept me home, and the television failed to alleviate my boredom.

The only justification for repetition is emphasis, as shown by Charles Dickens in the opening lines of *A Tale of Two Cities*.

> It was the best of times, it was the worst of times, it was the age of wisdom, it was the age of foolishness, it was the epoch of belief, it was the epoch of incredulity...

Both excerpts below are correct, but they vary in style.

The truly entertaining and illuminating new novel from world-famous author Wolf is on the must-read list in all the best local high schools and is the popular choice with numerous important book clubs.

Schools and book clubs recommend Wolf's new novel for education and entertainment.

Create variety in sentence structure and length. Follow a long sentence with a short one, for example.

An ominous and leering figure lurked in the shadows of the dumpsters at the far end of the alleyway. I ran.

No matter what style you adopt, do not let verbiage interfere with your objective. If your message hides amid pages of tedium, then it is lost forever.

Control Tense

There are three possible time frames – past, present, and future. These govern when the story happens relative to the reader. Within each, there are four tenses that tell when events happen relative to each other – the simple, perfect, progressive, and perfect progressive tenses.

Present Time Frame
I eat (simple present tense)
I have eaten (present perfect)
I am eating (present progressive)
I have been eating (present perfect progressive)

Past Time Frame
I ate (simple past tense)
I had eaten (past perfect)
I was eating (past progressive)
I had been eating (past perfect progressive)

Future Time Frame
I shall eat (simple future tense)
I shall have eaten (future perfect)
I shall be eating (future progressive)
I shall have been eating (future perfect progressive)

The general rule is to avoid transitions from one time frame to another. The following sentence jumps incorrectly from present to future to past.

> This book *is* (present) an attempt to help. The bulk of the book *will trace* (future) the lessons I *learned* (past).

Either the book is in existence, or it will be, but not both. Begin in one time frame and stay there.

Correct:

> This book *is* (present tense) an attempt to help. The bulk of the book *traces* (present tense) the lessons I *have learned* (present perfect tense).

Notice that the use of the present perfect tense, "have learned," allows the writer to reference a prior event while remaining in the present time frame.

In the example below, the writer begins in the past time frame but shifts incorrectly into the present and then back to the past.

> In his lecture last week, Mr. Smith *considered* (past) how the essay "Thoughts On Grammar" *has affected* (present perfect tense) its readers. Mr. Smith *quotes* (present) the essay's author, Ms. Wright, who *said* (past), "My goal is to help the language and those who speak it."

To correct, stay in the past time frame and use the past perfect tense to describe the events that predate the lecture.

Correct:

> In his lecture last week, Mr. Smith *considered* (past) how the essay "Thoughts On Grammar" *had affected* (past perfect) its readers. Mr. Smith *quoted* (past) the essay's author, Ms. Wright, who *had said* (past perfect), "My goal is to help the language and those who speak it."

There are a few exceptions to the general rule. Quoted material, such as Ms. Wright's comment in the above example, always appears verbatim.

Another exception is to recognize the ongoing relevance of

creative work by describing it in the present tense.

> I *wrote* a report last spring in which I *proposed* a new grammar curriculum. (The repeated past tense implies that the proposal lacks current significance.)

Correct:

> I *wrote* a report last spring in which I *propose* a new grammar curriculum. (The shift to the present time frame indicates the ongoing relevance of the report.)

Avoid Informality

When writing formally, avoid the pronouns "you," "me," "I," and "we," and avoid contractions, slang, and idiom. This produces a third-person narrative, which is the standard choice for formal prose.

<u>Informal:</u> *You* should never use the second-person pronoun.

<u>Formal:</u> *One* should never use the second-person pronoun.

Exceptions, of course, exist. The first-person and second-person pronouns work well for instructional manuals, like this one, and can create intimacy or levity.

From the opening sentence of *Moby Dick*, author Herman Melville appeals directly to the reader, and he sustains that bond throughout the novel. Notice how, in Chapter 72, Melville's choice of pronouns creates a light mood that offsets the danger that unfolds.

> You have seen Italian organ boys holding a dancing ape by a long cord. Just so, from the ship's steep side, did I hold Queequeg down there in the sea, by what is technically called in the fishery a monkey rope, attached to a strong strip of canvas belted round his waist. It was a humorously perilous business for both of us. For, before we proceed further, it must be said that the monkey rope was fast at both ends; fast to Queequeg's broad canvas belt, and fast to my narrow leather one. So that for better or for worse, we two, for the time, were wedded; and should poor Queequeg sink to rise no more, then both

> usage and honor demanded that instead of cutting the cord, it should drag me down in his wake.

J. D. Salinger achieves a close and confidential connection in *The Catcher in the Rye* by using not only a first-person narrator but also contractions and slang.

> If you really want to hear about it, the first thing you'll probably want to know is where I was born, and what my lousy childhood was like, and how my parents were occupied and all before they had me, and all that David Copperfield kind of crap, but I don't feel like going into it, if you want to know the truth.

Salinger's casual tone brings a light touch to a difficult subject and reflects a calculated purpose. If you decide to write in a casual style, then do so for a serious reason.

Lesson Twelve
Edit Thoroughly

No composition is error free, so allow plenty of time to review.

1. Know what your thesis is and state it clearly.
2. Delete any information that is irrelevant to the thesis.
3. Confine each paragraph to a single sub-thesis. Delete any irrelevant information or move it to an appropriate paragraph.
4. Review the fluidity of your transitions.
5. Remove passive voice and use compelling verbs.
6. Use modifiers only if they are informative and not redundant.
7. Review any change in time frame or tense.
8. Check grammar and punctuation.

Conclusion

The purpose of this book is to teach a correct set of rules. You will still face improper usage every day. People will say "me" when they should say "I" and "I" when they should say "me." You will hear "who" instead of "whom," "laid" instead of "lay," and "different than" instead of "different from." The goal is to recognize the mistakes when you hear them and to know how to fix them.

Appendix

I. Parts of Speech

The Basic Parts of Speech

Recognizing the part of speech of every word in a sentence will help you choose between the subject or object pronoun, for example, or between an adjective or an adverb, or a preposition or a conjunction.

Subject: The subject is the noun that performs the main action of the sentence or clause.

Predicate: The predicate states an action (action verb) or a state of being (linking verb).

Adjective: Adjectives modify nouns.

Adverb: An adverb answers the question *why*, *where*, *when*, or *how* and describes a verb, an adjective, or another adverb.

Predicate Nominative: A noun that follows a linking verb and re-identifies or renames the subject is a predicate nominative.

Predicate Adjective: An adjective that follows a linking verb and describes the subject is a predicate adjective.

Subject Complement: The subject complement is another name for the word or phrase that follows a linking verb and can be either a predicate nominative or a predicate adjective.

Direct Object: A direct object answers the question *whom* or *what* and is the direct recipient of the action.

Indirect Object: The indirect object participates indirectly in the action and is usually synonymous with a prepositional phrase. For example, "I wrote *her*" replaces "I wrote *to her*."

Preposition: A preposition precedes a prepositional object, and the resulting phrase, a *prepositional phrase*, modifies a word within the sentence.

Prepositional Object: This is the noun, noun clause, or pronoun that follows a preposition.

Conjunction: A conjunction joins two parallel structures or joins a dependent clause to an independent sentence.

Coordinating Conjunctions: These are the seven conjunctions – "and," "or," "nor," "for," "but," "yet," and "so" – that can join independent structures and therefore create compound subjects or objects, compound predicates, and compound sentences.

Subordinating Conjunctions: These are conjunctions that join a main clause with a dependent clause.

Determiner: Determiners "determine" the noun by modifying it to the specific, as in "*a* hat" and "*the* dog." Other determiners are "an," "this," "that," "these," and "those."

Pronoun: A pronoun stands in for a noun. The word itself means "on behalf of" the noun.

Possessive Modifiers: A possessive modifier is a pronoun that operates as a determiner. Examples are "my," "your," "his," "her," "their," and "our," as in "*my* hat."

Possessive Pronouns: Possessive pronouns are like possessive modifiers except that they can stand alone as nouns. Examples are "mine," "yours," "his," "hers," "theirs," and "ours," as in "the hat that is *mine*."

Appositive: The word "appositive" comes from the Latin word for "subsidiary." It is a noun or noun phrase that describes or identifies another noun within the sentence.

Participles, Gerunds, and Infinitives

These are verb forms that do not function as verbs but maintain some of the same traits as verbs. For example, they can be transitive or intransitive (the former need a direct object); they can be active or linking (the latter need a subject complement); and they can be modified only by an adverb or adverb phrase (not by an adjective).

Participles

A participle is a verb ending in "-ing" or "-ed" that serves as an adjective. The *present participle* ends in "-ing" and the *past participle* ends in "-ed."

The *aspiring* singer takes voice lessons. (present participle)

The *reheated* coffee is tasteless. (past participle)

Many past participles are irregular, which means they do not end in "-ed." Examples are *gone, risen, been, become, done, drunk, bid,* and *bet*. There are no irregular present participles, but in a few cases the spelling of the verb changes to accommodate the "-ing" suffix. Examples are "lying" (from "lie") and "dying" (from "die").

Lying on the couch, I can just make out the *risen* sun.

Do not confuse a participle, which is an adjective, with the verb that is the same word. Which sentence below contains a participle?

My children are grown.

My children are growing.

My children have grown.

The first contains the past participle "grown," which functions as a predicate adjective following a linking verb. In the other two sentences, the participle forms are the present progressive verb "are growing" and the present perfect tense "have grown."

Gerunds

A gerund is a verb in the present participle form (one that ends in "-ing") that acts as a noun. A gerund can fulfill any noun role.

Reading is a quiet activity. (The gerund is the subject.)

My favorite activity is *playing* squash. (The gerund is the predicate nominative.)

Did you enjoy *watching* the race? (The gerund is the direct object.)

Do you give *playing* regularly the credit for your success? (The gerund is the indirect object.)

For better *balancing*, tighten your stomach muscles. (The gerund is the prepositional object.)

Infinitives

An infinitive is a root verb and can operate as a noun, an adjective, or an adverb.

>*To err* is human. (The infinitive can be the subject.)

>Your duty is *to wash* the dishes. (predicate nominative)

>I prefer *to watch* television. (direct object)

>Reading is an activity *to do* at home. (adjective)

>He came *to visit* me. (adverb)

Not all infinitive phrases begin with the word "to." In certain sentence constructions, the "to" either drops from the infinitive or is optional.

>Let *go*.

>I helped *bake* it.

>She had better *ask*.

Modal verbs also precede a bare infinitive. Modal verbs are those with one conjugation and one mood, such as "must," "may," "should," "can," and "could."

>You may *eat*.

>I should *leave*.

>She must *go*.

How to Use Participles, Gerunds, and Infinitives

A verb form retains the requirements of a verb, even though it functions as another part of speech within the sentence. For example, use an adverb, not an adjective, to modify a verb form.

>*To think quickly* is an asset. ("To think" is the subject, modified by the adverb "quickly.")

>*Exiting quietly and with haste from the cinema when one must leave early* is wise. (Use an adverb or adverb phrase to modify the gerund "exiting.")

If a verb form is transitive, it must contain a direct object.

> *Playing* squash, I hurt my ankle.
>
> *Riding* horses is fun.
>
> He loves *to watch* soccer.

If the underlying verb is intransitive, there is no direct object.

> *Biking*, I hurt my foot.
>
> My favorite pastime is *swimming*.
>
> I love *to cook*.

If the underlying verb is a linking verb, then the verb form must precede a subject complement.

> *Sounding* anxious, she cried for help. ("Sounding" is the participle form of the linking verb "to sound," and "anxious" is a predicate adjective.)
>
> I love *smelling* like soap after a shower. ("Smelling" is the gerund form of the linking verb, and "like soap" is a predicate adjective.)
>
> Why does it have *to be* my mother who chaperones at the prom? ("To be" is the infinitive form of a linking verb, and "my mother" is a predicate nominative.)

If the underlying verb is a linking verb, and if it is followed by a predicate nominative that is a pronoun, then use the subject form of the pronoun.

Incorrect:

> *Being her*, she scored highest on the test. (The linking verb is a participle and needs a subject-form pronoun to create a predicate nominative.)
>
> Would you prefer *being him*? (The linking verb is a gerund and needs a subject-form pronoun.)
>
> It had *to be me*. (The linking verb is an infinitive and needs a subject-form pronoun.)

Correct:

>*Being she*, she scored highest on the test. ("She" is correct to create a predicative nominative.)

>Would you prefer *being he*? ("He" is correct to create a predicative nominative.)

>It had *to be I*. ("I" is correct as the predicative nominative.)

II. Sample Sentences

There is one left.

"There" is an adverb, which describes the verb "is" (a linking verb). "One" is the subject, and "left" is an irregular past participle that serves as the predicate adjective.

They gave me one.

"They" is the subject, "gave" is a transitive verb whose direct object is "one," and "me" is an indirect object (synonymous with "to me").

I shall dine tonight with Tim but not Sue.

"I" is the subject, and "shall dine" is the predicate (future tense). "Tonight" is an adverb, "with" a preposition, and "Tim but not Sue" is a compound prepositional object.

He requests that the one to drive home tonight be I.

The main clause is "He requests." The noun clause that follows is the direct object. The verb "requests" is an action of contingency, so the noun clause requires the subjunctive form of the verb. The infinitive "be" is the correct subjunctive form. "One" is the subject of the dependent clause, and the subject complement is "I," which makes correct use of the subject pronoun. The infinitive "to drive" acts as an adjective. "Home" and "tonight" are adverbs that describe the action "drive."

Will it be Sue or he attending?

"It" is the subject; "will be" is the predicate. "Sue or he" is a compound predicate nominative. "Attending" is a participle.

Playing basketball is what he does best.

"Playing" is a gerund and serves as the subject. "Basketball" is the direct object of the gerund. "Is" is a linking verb, and the noun clause "what he does best" is a predicate nominative.

My son is not as tall as the other player.

"My son is tall" is the main clause in this comparison. Its structure is subject - linking verb - predicate adjective. "Not" is an adverb that describes the first occurrence of "as," and "as," in that spot, is an adverb that describes "tall." The second "as" is a conjunction that begins the subordinate clause, which is the parallel comparison of the main clause except that the redundant elements – the verb and the adjective – drop off.

If I were free, I could join you.

"I could" is the main clause (uses a modal verb). "Join" is an infinitive (without the "to") and is the direct object of "could." "You" is the direct object of "join." "If" introduces a subordinate clause, within which "I" is the subject, "were" is the predicate (in the subjunctive form), and "free" is a predicate adjective.

III. Sentence Diagramming

Follow these steps to transform words into a picture.

1. On a horizontal line, place the subject on the left and the predicate on the right. Then separate the two with a vertical line that crosses through the horizontal line.

2. After the verb, write its direct object, if it has one, on the horizontal line. Divide the verb and the object with a vertical line that stops at the horizontal line.

3. For predicate adjectives and predicate nominatives, place them as you would a direct object, but draw the vertical line slanting to the left (back to the subject).

4. Place all modifiers and determiners on diagonal lines slanted to the right below the words they modify.

5. For two modifiers joined by a conjunction, connect the modifiers with a horizontal dotted line and write the conjunction on the dotted line.

6. Begin a prepositional phrase by placing the preposition on a slanted line beneath the modified word. Next write the prepositional object on a horizontal line that projects from the bottom right of the slant. Treat indirect objects the same except leave the slanted line blank.

7. To create a compound subject, a compound predicate, or a compound object, connect two horizontal lines with a dotted vertical line and place the conjunction on the vertical line.

8. To create a compound sentence, connect two horizontal lines with a dotted vertical line that has a horizontal step. Place the conjunction on the step.

9. For a modifying clause, first, draw a dotted slanted line beneath the modified word and write the conjunction, if there is one, on the dotted line. Next, draw a detached horizontal line below the slanted line and place the clause on the horizontal line.

10. To add a noun clause, use a pedestal to elevate the clause on its own horizontal line. If a conjunction begins the clause, then draw a dotted vertical line above the verb and write the conjunction on top. Draw an infinitive phrase the same way, except add a right-slanting downward line before the verb that marginally crosses the horizontal. If the infinitive includes "to," then write it on the slanting line.

11. With gerunds and participles, write the verb form on a downward slope that ends in a horizontal line. For gerunds use a downward step, and for participles use a bent line. Place a subject complement or a direct object, if there is one, on the horizontal line.

12. Place an appositive in parentheses next to the noun it identifies.

It helps to look at an example.

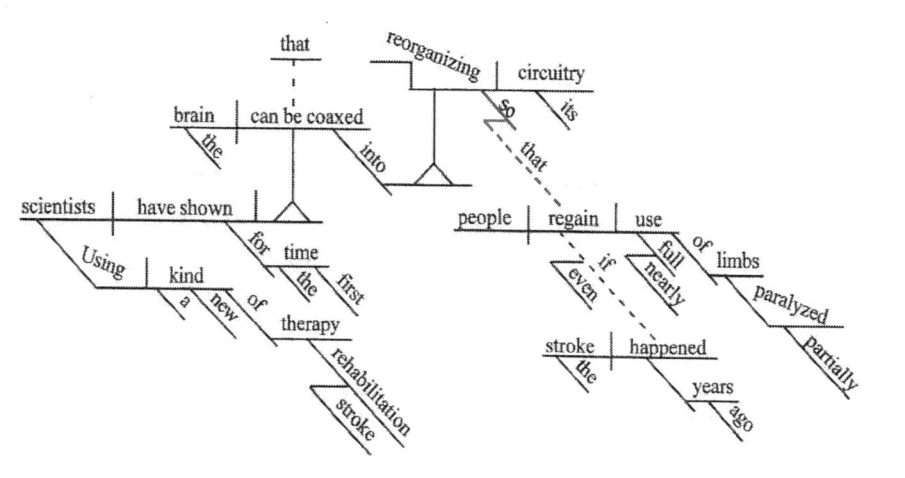

"Scientists" is the subject, and "have shown" is the predicate. The noun clause "that the brain can be coaxed" is the direct object. The noun clause sits on a pedestal, connected by the conjunction "that." The other two conjunctions, "that" and "if," join subordinate clauses that modify the words above them. Notice that each of the four clauses – the main clause plus the three dependent clauses – sit on horizontal lines. The gerund "reorganizing" slants down a step, and the participles "using" and "paralyzed" slope down bent lines. "Circuitry" and "kind" are the direct objects of "reorganizing" and "using."

Here is the full sentence.

> Using a new kind of stroke rehabilitation therapy, scientists have shown for the first time that the brain can be coaxed into reorganizing its circuitry so that people regain nearly full use of partially paralyzed limbs even if the stroke happened years ago.

Can you prove your mastery of the language by identifying the part of speech for each word in the sentence below (adapted from James Madison's inaugural address of 1809)?

> It has long been the true glory of the United States, indulging no passions that trespass on the rights or the repose of other nations, to cultivate peace by observing

justice and to entitle America to the respect of the nations at war by fulfilling with the most scrupulous impartiality her neutral obligations.

It – subject
has been – predicate (present perfect tense)
long – adverb
the – determiner
true – adjective
glory – predicate nominative
of – preposition
the – determiner
United States – object of the preposition
indulging – adjective (participle)
passions – direct object of the participle
no – adjective
that – relative pronoun
trespass – verb
on – preposition (begins a compound prepositional object)
the – determiner
rights – object of the preposition (first part)
or – conjunction
the – determiner
repose – object of the preposition (second part)
of – preposition
other – adjective
nations – object of the preposition
to cultivate – infinitive (begins a compound appositive)
peace – direct object of the infinitive
by – preposition
observing – object of the preposition (gerund)
justice – direct object of the gerund
and – conjunction
to entitle – infinitive (completes the compound appositive)
America – direct object of the infinitive
to – preposition
the – determiner
respect – object of the preposition
of – preposition
the – determiner
nations – object of the preposition
at – preposition

war -- object of the preposition
by – preposition
fulfilling – object of the preposition (gerund)
with – preposition
the – determiner
most – adverb
scrupulous – adjective
impartiality – object of the preposition
her – possessive pronoun (references "America")
neutral – adjective
obligations – direct object of the gerund "fulfilling"

See the following page for the diagram.

64

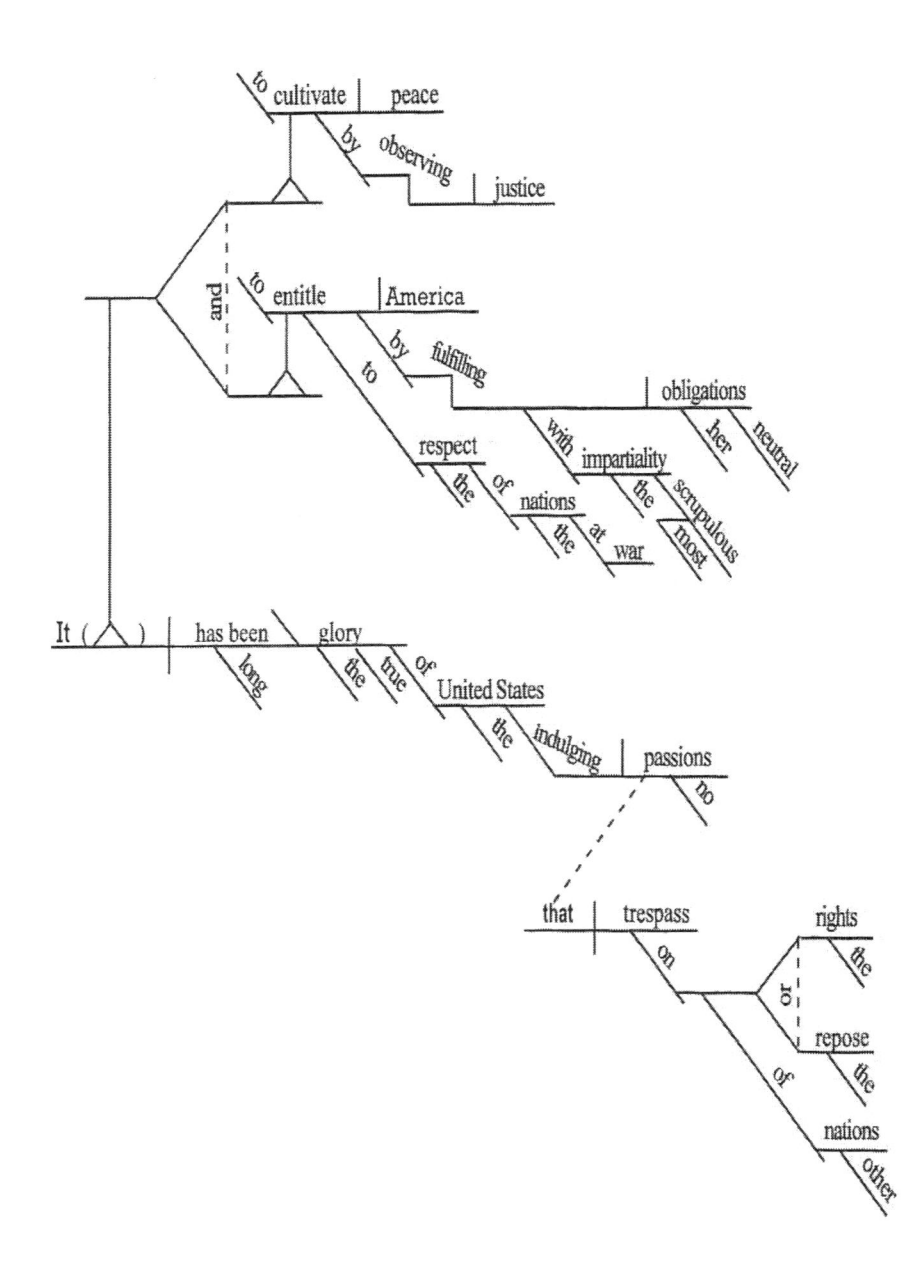

Made in the USA
Columbia, SC
22 February 2025